OVERTHROW

10 WAYS TO TELL A CHALLENGER STORY

ADAM MORGAN
AND
MARK HOLDEN

phd & eatbigfish.

INTRODUCTION

INTRODUCTION: THE TROUBLE WITH 'CHALLENGER BRAND'

Anyone interested in challengers is interested in compression: how do you make a story utterly compelling in a very short space of time? And one of the reasons that the concept of the 'challenger brand' has caught on, you might argue, is that it itself does just that: within just two words you surely have all the ingredients of an engaging story – conflict, a protagonist and an adversary, an anticipation of a future event whose outcome is uncertain, the new order against the establishment. It's all there.

Except that it isn't. Not really. Because for all that people talk more than they ever did about challenger brands (3,020,000 hits in 0.11 seconds on Google this morning), all too often it is the clichéd and superficial view of what a challenger narrative actually is that persists: either 'little brand explicitly calling out big brand' (think Avis or Ryanair) or 'turn every category rule on its head' (think the young Red Bull or Grameen Bank).

But if we look at a new generation of challengers from the last ten years, do they really all fall into one of those two different approaches? A new generation, spanning South Africa to Uruguay to the US, from automotive to betting to beer to tech, with marketing spends ranging from millions of dollars to nothing at all – would they all really be about just one of these two narratives?

There seemed to us to be an opportunity to learn from this new challenger generation, and put on the table a more evolved model of what it means to be a challenger. What if we were to group all the different challengers from the last ten years into the ten most common challenger stories they tell? What if we were to identify for each of them what (not whom) they were challenging, and how they were doing it? What if we then interviewed a shining example to get an insight on what it really meant to live in that narrative? What if we could unpack the communications implications for each?

GOOD IDEA, WE THOUGHT.
LET'S DO IT.
SO HERE IT IS.

HOW THIS BOOK WORKS

There are eleven chapters in the book. In the first ten, we will explore each of these challenger narratives, one chapter at a time. In each case we'll open the chapter with the key characteristics of that narrative, followed by an interview with one of the most interesting contemporary examples of a challenger occupying this space. Each chapter will then move on to explore what kinds of communications strategy are most powerful for a challenger brand with this narrative as an ambition.

The thinking in the book is intended to be not simply a typology, but a coherent model that represents a usable tool. And so the last chapter will focus on how to use this model, whether you are an existing challenger looking to refresh your consumer relationship, or a new player searching for a fresh way into a cluttered market.

We have done much more research around this new model than we can fit into this slim volume. If you are interested, you can find directions to more reference material available in the Postscript at the end of the book.

CONTENTS PAGE

PUBLISHED BY PHD

The Telephone Exchange
5 North Crescent
Chenies Street
London
WC1E 7PH

www.phdww.com

First published 2012

Copyright © PHD Worldwide

Lead author:
Adam Morgan, Founder of eatbigfish

Co-authors:
Mark Holden, Malcolm Devoy and
Hugh Cameron, PHD Worldwide

Design:
Sangers & Mash

Illustrations:
Becca Thorne

1. THE PEOPLE'S CHAMPION

The People's Champion makes a very specific claim: that it is a challenger standing up for the consumer, who has been undeservedly – and perhaps even cynically – exploited by the establishment players in the category so far. The People's Champion is fighting to succeed because, it says, in doing so the real winner is you, the consumer – and if we both join together we can overcome the cynical fat cats that have been lining their pockets at your expense until now.

An increasingly popular narrative in a number of categories, we're starting to see some important variations on the overall theme, of which we will look at just a couple here. The first is where the brand takes it upon itself to stand up for the people, or a particular group of people. Virgin, for example, has historically tended to seek to occupy this space as a matter of course when entering a category: it always chooses to pick a fight with the way the category or the market leader is currently serving its customers – and always, it claims, on the people's behalf. Charles Schwab famously champions Main Street, rather than Wall Street.

The second, more recent variation in the way the People's Champion is used is obviously where the brand is 'of the people' in a rather different sense – namely in that it presents itself as a conduit for

people themselves to collectively and collaboratively solve an issue that needs addressing. Most of the Open Source and emerging 'collective creative' brands (commercial, political and philanthropic) are occupying this space – the latter being brands where the consumer either comes up with, and/or chooses the answers themselves. HopeLab's Ruckus Nation would be an example of where the people create possible solutions to a societal goal – the incentivised development of a branded toy to help tackle child obesity by getting middle schoolers off the couch, where anyone can submit the winning answer. And Linux bridges both these two meanings of being The People's Champion, in the stance it takes on giving people control over their software, in opposition to Microsoft, and in the way that it does it, through Open Source.

Summary of this Narrative

Core Strategic Thought:
A challenger that consciously sets itself up as on the side of the consumer, often specifically against the 'cynical'/ fat cat market leader.

What is it challenging? The motives and interests of the market leader.

Why does its consumer respond to it? 'They are fighting for me; if they win, I win'.

INTERVIEW WITH HEIDI BRAUER, CMO OF KULULA AIRLINES

Kulula was the pioneer low cost airline in South Africa, competing for local traffic against the established giant that was South African Airlines. To succeed, it focused on a few key routes, and looked to persuade a new generation of South Africans to fly, and fly kulula because it was an airline for them. Consistently breakthrough challenger marketing has allowed the brand to grow to a twenty percent share in a fiercely competitive market, and stay a strong number two in overall passenger numbers to SAA, despite two further low cost launches in its wake.

Interview:

Q: Who is kulula for?

HB: I think kulula is a brand for the people and that's what we started as. We said: 'South Africans, you deserve to fly, and let's make it affordable for you, and let's make it easy for you'. I mean, that's our name, kulula – it means 'easily' – so let's make it pleasant for you, and let's make it accessible from an experience point of view so that not only is it affordable, but when you're on board you feel comfortable. You can't do that whilst delivering it from a snobby place, because then there's a disconnect. And so we've always been for the people, for South Africa.

Q: How does this challenger position of being 'for the people' translate into brand behaviour?

HB: We've always fought for things that are important to South Africans, things that are affordable, charities that are relevant. We've supported South African satire in the form of ZA News, which nobody else would support because we are authentically behind South Africans. And being authentic enables you to do things and test things and create things that are a little edgier and that are a little riskier, because you're doing them in a context that is honest.

Q: Can you give an example of kulula being 'for the people'?

HB: In 2010 we had the Soccer World Cup in South Africa, and what happened was the airlines were all being accused of putting up the prices.

So we decided to put out an ad, a print ad in the newspapers, to say 'Actually, it is affordable to fly, and here are some prices'. It would have been nuts to ignore the fact that it was the Soccer World Cup, but there were very strict FIFA rules and regulations about what you could and couldn't say or show, but we're kulula and we push things a little. So we pushed things a little and we had the odd soccer ball and we had the odd reference to 2010, and so on.

Believe me, we consulted the guidelines, which were thick, but we also knew we were on the thin edge of the wedge. So we put this beautifully hand illustrated ad into the Sunday paper first, and it was to follow in the dailies. It was a pricing ad, and no sooner had it gone out and was due for its appearance in the dailies, when I got a phone call from our legal department, our internal legal department, and our lawyer said to me – I felt like I was 16 again – "Heidi ! What have you done?!" And I had this mixture of elation, because I knew exactly what it meant. It meant we were in trouble with FIFA, and I was thrilled. Because that's what kulula does, we challenge.

I knew we weren't in that much trouble. From a lawyer's point of view probably we were, but from a brand point of view it was such an opportunity to be for the people again, because the people at the time in South Africa were just up to here with being told that 'We can't use 2010' – gosh, we were in 2010. 'We couldn't use soccer balls' – gosh, everybody was playing soccer. It was just getting ludicrous.

So what did we do? Well, we needed to keep going on about pricing so our team at our ad agency came up with an ad then that took out all of the symbolism and wordage that we were supposedly not allowed to use and replaced it, but in the cheekiest, cheekiest way, and that was just the perfect balance of being cheeky, taking risk and being honestly and authentically kulula, and South Africa and the world loved us for it. Because only kulula could do that – because kulula is for the people, for South Africa, a challenger, a supporter, and all of those things rolled into one.

We got worldwide recognition and kulula is known around the world as this little airline that could.

So those are the kinds of things that kulula does, and if there's a cause outside of air travel or outside of travel that is meaningful for South Africans, kulula will support it.

Communications Behaviour

"THE PEOPLE'S CHAMPION SHOULD FOCUS ON CREATING CAMPAIGNS THAT ARE ALSO NEWS STORIES – THEREFORE CREATIVE, MEDIA AND PR INTEGRATION IS ESSENTIAL.

THEY SHOULD LOOK TO USE SOCIAL CHANNELS TO UNITE PEOPLE BEHIND CAUSES. THEY SHOULD ALSO EXPLORE THE POSSIBILITIES OF HAVING A SPOKESPERSON (FOUNDER/CEO FOR EXAMPLE) TO LEAD THE CAUSE"

The most important communication principle for the People's Champion is to tell the truth. This is how this challenger defines itself against the established companies or brands within the category.

It is therefore very important for this challenger to practice open communication. And, of course, one of the most important elements of open communications is listening to people. A company or brand in this position would ensure social media monitoring is used to actually shape the product and marketing strategy – responding, when appropriate, to what people are asking for. They should respond to key individuals – harnessing the influence of their followers as a group that is 'helping shape the movement.'

They should attempt to respond within mainstream communications, in order to reach a significant amount of the target audience, but also within the communication channels that the 'people' use – typically these may be microblogging and social network sites.

These social environments should be used to steer the momentum – feeding people with the company's manifesto and constantly re-engaging with them by responding and re-tweeting pertinent tweets/status updates.

They should seek to arm their followers with information to rebel against the established order. In order to do this, the People's Champion would need an armoury of content at their disposal. Therefore a content strategy becomes a priority – content that provides information packaged in a compelling and concise manner and with social plug-ins to make it easy for people to share.

Being controversial can pay back dividends for the People's Champion, so they often create a stir to get people talking. To that end, PR, social media, content creation and media should be aligned to increase the likelihood that campaigns become genuinely PR-able news stories.

People's Champion brands will sometimes elect a company spokesperson (frequently the founder or CEO) to deliver this unified message. The right individual must have an authentic belief in the cause and is prepared to be an external face. Having a spokesperson taps into the behavioural economic principle of source credibility. This is where people tend to accept the point of view from sources they consider to be trustworthy: Having an inspirational leader that people believe in will allow the messaging to garner greater credibility.

Essentials for the People's Champion:

- Maintain an honest dialogue

- Provide engaging content and respond to the feedback

- Communicate through the same means as the people, such as social networking sites

- Create newsworthy communications

- Consider installing a spokesperson for the cause

2.
THE
MISSIONARY

2. THE MISSIONARY

The Missionary is a challenger with a transparent sense of purpose. It is a group of people who see themselves as agents of change, a force for good, and who wear that bigger purpose with pride and ambition, inviting others to identify with it and share in it. The Missionary challenges what it wants to actively change in the world around it, particularly in the category itself, often because it believes it to be ethically or ideologically wrong.

Al Jazeera is a good example of this kind of challenger. Its mantra is 'The opinion and the other opinion': pushing back against what it feels for too long has been a one-sided portrayal of events in the Middle East by the Western media, it is on a mission to redress that balance. If the West feels Al Jazeera's coverage is sometimes one-sided, their response is that the West's has been one-sided for years, failing to report the real tragedy beneath the headlines, and flinching from the tough questions when interviewing their own Western leaders. And Al Jazeera's mission goes further, as their involvement in the Arab Spring demonstrated: in the real world, beyond the media world, they see themselves as promoting peaceful protest and advancing the cause of human rights.

Not every challenger, let alone every brand, needs to have a sense of purpose. But the Missionary does – and it is this larger ambition that we emotionally attach ourselves to, or choose deliberately to walk past, as human beings as much as consumers. As such, the Missionary's key challenges lie in how to actively wake up and re-educate a broader audience than those who are already alive to its point of view, and in doing so, create opportunities for a deeper and engaged dialogue around its philosophy and ambitions.

Summary of this Narrative

Core Strategic Thought:
A challenger fired up with a view about the world it has to share, wearing a strong sense of purpose on its sleeve.

What is it challenging? The belief system or foundations underpinning the category the way the category has thought and behaved to date.

Why does its consumer respond to it? Identification with the challenger's beliefs about category (and the way category ought to fit within the wider world).

INTERVIEW WITH DAVID HIEATT, CO-FOUNDER OF HIUT DENIM

David and Clare Hieatt are serial entrepreneurs, whose clothing ventures have included the creation of howies, a highly regarded apparel company acquired by Timberland in 2006. David and Claire have just launched Hiut Denim, a challenger jeans brand on a mission.

As with Newcastle Brown Ale and Lark in later chapters, we have chosen here to focus on a challenger very early in its life, one just starting to tell its unique story and build its community. Here David talks about the mission his new brand is on, how challengers need to think if they want to create big change, and the importance of really working out your 'Why'.

Interview:

Q: Who you are you and what you do?

DH: My name is David Hieatt. I am, I guess, an entrepreneur, which means I run businesses, mostly because I'm unemployable. But I run the Do Lectures. I started a company called Howies and sold it and left. And now I am running Hiut Denim and we make jeans in Cardigan, Wales. And we're going to build a nice, small global denim company that tries to change a few things.

Q: What was the inspiration for starting the company?

DH: I suppose the inspiration started with me walking out of my last company, when I closed the door, walked down the steps and went, "what am I going to do now?"

The other thing is I live in this town that knows how to make jeans, for three to four decades it made 35,000 pairs of jeans a week every week, and one day had to stop and all that skill remained here with no one to show how good it was.

Imagine if you got good at something over a 20-year period and then I said to you 'Guess what? You can't do it anymore'. Whether you're a photographer or a journalist or a writer, just when you got really good at it, somebody said to you, right, put your pen down, put the camera down, you can't do it anymore. I felt like that's what this town was told: you can't make jeans anymore, although you've gotten really good at it.

I knew I wanted to go and start a jeans brand because I had fallen slightly geekily in love with jeans. And it seemed obvious at the time to try and make them here – the people are out there and they've got knowledge of making jeans. If you're going to go and start a jeans company anywhere, actually, Cardigan is the place – it's the hot spot of denim.

So, it was obvious for me to try and pull the love of the town, the love of jeans and my ability to go and start businesses together into almost three circles; in that circle where they all meet is where the Hiut Denim Company sits.

Q: How much was the idea for the company led by the business case, versus this sense of injustice you feel for the people who lost their jobs here?

DH: I left howies and I wrote a business plan for jeans and I showed it to my investor and they said "this is brilliant, let's go", but I thought, there's something missing here. We're defined by not what we do, but why we do it, and for me, I couldn't work out why I was going to go and start this thing again.

I knew I could do it, I had gotten sufficiently good at what I was doing to be able to go and play with the big boys, but I hadn't worked out my why. Then I got a phone call from Gideon, the old jeans designer, asking "why aren't you doing the plan? It's a great plan." And I said, well, I haven't worked out why. And he said, "well, I thought it was about getting the town making jeans again?"

That was the moment where you just go, of course! That's the why. We're going to go and try and get 400 people their jobs back. That's why we want to go and start a great global denim company, because the skill is in this town, the skill never left the town. The economics made the factory leave, not the fact that they weren't good at it.

I think we need to understand our purpose, without that we're just going to set up a company to make money to sell it. In a way, businesses need soul too and the 'why' is the soul.

Q: Do you feel that your ambition to get the town making jeans again ties into a wider concern for a lack of British manufacturing?

DH: We live in an age where manufacturing goes away but doesn't come back. I want to resist that temptation to go, well, it always goes away. I want to show that we can make things, we can design things and we can put ideas into things and we can do it from here – and I want to combine all those things to show that actually Britain needs to make things more. We need to be better at design and ideas. This notion that we can't make anything has to be disproved.

The other thing we have to prove is that you can actually make it in this town and be a success and be a global denim company. Britain is not very good at thinking big. I think it thinks too small. What we need is lots of people like myself or other entrepreneurs who actually don't understand why we can't compete with the best. We have great ideas, we understand great design and we can make things. We can't probably be the cheapest at things, but our area of expertise means that we can be the best. So, to win, we have to operate here.

There was a really interesting moment in the banking crisis where there was a collective unease. We got worried because we found out how vulnerable we were. If you can't trust the service industry and we don't make anything, what do we do as a country? What's our purpose? Britain at that point said to itself, do you know what? We need to make more stuff here more.

So, the bigger question of can we show that Britain can do it? There's definitely no doubt in my mind that we can.

Q: How do you reach the level of influence necessary to make a change in the world?

DH: I think it's almost two steps. Initially, you need your 1,000 true fans, the people who get what you're doing, are going to support you, will always be there for you. And if you don't go beyond the 1,000 true fans, you've got a nice, small little business, but essentially you're going to have to go beyond that if you're going to go into the mainstream.

The biggest change comes from the mainstream. So, if you're just going to hide yourself on the margins and you want to go and try and change things, I don't think you do it really from the edge.

I think it's important for the best, authentic, genuine companies to have a story. I also think that they have to tell it particularly well. For us, we are jeans makers, but we have to be every bit as good at being great storytellers too, because we have to get our story out there. The story has to be true. It has to connect with the customer.

Q: Who do you see as your competition and what other companies do you respect within the category?

DH: I think Nudie over in Scandinavia do Nudie well. I think they make them in Italy, which is interesting. I think they've set out their stall in terms of their principles, I think they do that well. In terms of other competition, there are millions of jeans brands – I'm just really interested in the ones that have a higher purpose where they actually want to use their company to go and do things as well as make things.

Q: How has business been in these first few months?

DH: Well, we've been going two and a half months. In the first week, we sold two month's worth of jeans. So we've got some nice problems to solve. At the moment, we've had to stop taking orders on the site because we can't really cope – we can only make ten pairs of jeans a day. We're trying to hire some more people. So it's going well, but there's a long way to go.

Q: What advice would you give to a brand trying to find its 'why?'

DH: I think you've got to tell your story and tell it well, and you've got to make sure that it resonates, both with yourself and your consumer. I mean, if you don't feel it, then I'm not sure you're going to get anybody else to feel it. I think that's the important thing: it's got to come from within you, but it has to be something quite big. It has be something that the customer thinks is a common problem.

Our plan for the first year or two years is really just find our feet. But I think for us the answer is ideas – we have to go and change something.

"THE MISSIONARY SHOULD CRYSTALLISE AND GRAPHICALLY REPRESENT THE KEY MESSAGE AND THEN BROADCAST IN ENVIRONMENTS THAT ALLOW FOR LONGER-FORM MESSAGE DELIVERY. THEY MUST BE A ZEALOT AND RESTLESS. THEY MUST CONSTANTLY REFRESH CREATIVE AROUND KEY THEMES (BUT KEEPING THE CORE MESSAGE CONSISTENT)."

When an individual goes about a mission to "right a wrong" in their personal life, they systematically build a case. Firstly, they might tell people close to them. They might get them on side and allow them to feel part of a group determined to collectively overturn the injustice. They may try to gain the support of other people that also feel passionately about the cause to stand together, in this mission.

And that is exactly how the Missionary goes about their plight. The Missionary campaigns for people to see the light. They seek to create a movement.

If the Missionary business or brand is about to launch, they might start within grass-roots channels and expand out from there. If they are already established they may go back to the grass-roots to deepen a connection at that level.

In order to galvanise people around the cause, a graphical image to represent the movement might be utilised – this would be a distinctive image that is easily recognisable. This would then be propagated across all touch points.

Messaging might be aligned around relevant stories – this can be done by the use of contextual advertising online. The Missionary might also build in a quick-response capability so that they can respond to relevant news stories with tactical messages.

Where a Missionary brand has an extended message to communicate, they should consider using channels that allow for longer-form message delivery. In this instance they should link all Paid communications to their Owned environments, where they can unfold more of the message.

They should also link their Paid communications to Earned environments where people can rally behind the cause – this could take the form of running a distinctive hashtag within all of their Paid communications which will direct people to witness, and contribute to, the movement happening within microblogs.

Branded-assets should be created that can be socialised by people that are getting behind the cause.

A brand with a Missionary narrative will never allow a message to fatigue – although the core message may remain the same, they should keep refreshing its expression.

Essentials for the Missionary:

- Start on a local level and build a momentum

- Have an opinion and constantly refresh creative to deliver it

- Be where the established competitors are and use channels that allow for longer-form messages to be delivered

- Use contextual advertising to marry message to topical themes

3. THE DEMOCRATISER

"**O**nce and forever, we have decided to side with the many', wrote Ingvar Kamprad, in 'The World is full of Opportunities', an internal guide for IKEA employees. From early in its life its founder wanted IKEA, in effect, to democratise.

As a challenger, the Democratiser believes in taking not from the 'rich' and giving to the 'poor', but taking from the 'few' and giving to the 'many' – opening up the beauty of great design, or the latest catwalk clothing, or the ability to become a broadcaster or news editor, and making it available to everyone. Sometimes this is done with an overtly idealistic flag flying above it (Current TV), sometimes without (Zara and Target). It is often characterised by remarkable pricing (surprisingly low or free) and/or the deliberate sharing of knowledge that was previously only known by a few. It challenges elitism, in effect. One might see TED as just such a democratiser, for example, sharing the world's greatest thinkers and concepts with anyone with a thirst for ideas and knowledge.

Being such a Democratiser frequently demands not just the development of entirely new business models, but also the fostering of a culture which makes a habit of asking different kinds of questions, questions that constantly provoke the identification of new opportunities and possibilities. It is said, for instance, that when Kamprad was first looking to create well-designed affordable furniture, instead of creating designs and then looking at how to make them cheaply, he went to lumberyards and looked at the most regular shapes of their discarded offcuts. It was around those shapes that he then built his designs – because it was the fact that they were made essentially from waste that then allowed him to produce items at a jaw-droppingly affordable price for his 'many' consumers.

The interview below looks at arguably one of the most important Democratisers in the world today – One Laptop Per Child. Their importance lies not simply in the nature of their ambition, and the value they create, but also – for us – in the example they represent of a Democratiser sometimes needing to motivate and harness other forces (strategic partnerships, governments) to realise their ambition.

Summary of this Narrative

Core Strategic Thought:
A challenger that takes something previously exclusive (stylish, luxurious, expensive, hi tech), and makes it much more broadly available to the masses.

What is it challenging? 'Elitism', the idea that something should be available only to the privileged or wealthy.

Why does its consumer respond to it? The brand has given them access to a world that they hadn't thought accessible to them.

INTERVIEW WITH RODRIGO ARBOLEDA – ONE LAPTOP PER CHILD

OLPC is an organisation set up to give every child in the world equal access to knowledge. Chaired by Nicholas Negroponte, they are best known to many for the technology that they have created to enable their ambition, and in particular their famous $100 laptop. But the aim of the Movement as a whole is, as Rodrigo Arboleda describes below, not about cheap technology but social equality. At the time of writing they had reached 2.5 million children in 41 countries, in 21 different languages.

Rodrigo Arboleda is the chairman and the chief executive officer of the One Laptop Per Child Association.

Interview:

Q: What is the idea behind One Laptop Per Child?

RA: It is very simple: it's to provide children in developing nations with at least the same initial access to knowledge, in quality and in quantity, as the most privileged child of New York, London, Tokyo or Berlin. Ten years ago, fifteen years ago, this could not have been possible. With the advent of the internet and the advent of digital age technologies, this aspiration can be fulfilled, and a child in a remote village in the agricultural sectors of the Amazon can have right now at least the same opportunity of access, as we have already demonstrated, to knowledge in quantity and in quality as the most privileged child in New York.

Q: Please explain how you came to see programming as so important to education

RA: In 1967, Seymour Papert was hired by MIT, together with another scientist by the name of Marvin Minsky, to start what would become a very well-renowned laboratory; it was the Artificial Intelligence Lab. And he arrived at MIT coming from working with Jean Piaget in learning the brain and how the brain learned. And he gave a declaration at the time that was a very controversial one. He said, well, empowering the child to learn is so important that one of these days every child should have a computer, because by learning to programme, a child learns four specific words of the dictionary and of the learning process that are critical.

One is critical thinking; if you have a programme that doesn't work and you need to debug a programme, you need to acquire critical thinking to understand what the hell has gone wrong with the programme.

The second one is the discipline to look for solutions,which is what everybody these days in programming has learned by repeating endlessly, trying to find out where he missed a comma or a little space here or there. So that discipline of searching for solutions is very important in the mind of a learning environment.

The third one is sharing. Until then, individual learning was considered to be the norm. In the programming environment, when you in desperation couldn't debug a programme, you ask around your fellow guys, hey, I'm going crazy with this, it doesn't work. The sharing became a very important element.

And finally, when you hopefully debug the programme and the programme works, you have to step back a little bit and reflect. So, critical thinking, solution-oriented mentality, sharing and reflection became four important words, not only in the environment of what was called at the time linear programming, that could be developed – and that could only happen if you had a computer.

Q: Tell us a little about how the laptop came to be developed

RA: We saw that the digital age technologies provided everything [we might need], but there was a cost. Seven years ago, say in 2005, a laptop was over probably $1,000, at least. So, we said, we need to reduce it to one-tenth, more or less – we need to try to reach a $100 laptop if we want to really be able to comply with the capacity of governments to provide education.

It forced us to take the heroic decision to make it for a child in a low-cost country – reducing [the spec] to the minimum requirements for a child of five years of age and getting rid of the superfluous fat that normal computers have. In your normal life you don't use more than 5% of the capacity of this computer; everything else is for the super genius, super high-end engineers that need thousands of calculations per second and so forth. We, the normal guys, don't need 90% of what the power here is. So, reducing that is a way to reduce the costs.

Q: Where do you sacrifice and where do you overcommit in order to increase your chances of success?

RA: We focus on primary school; that's where you can mould the brain of a child. For us to change the brain of a child in high school is too costly in terms of time, energy, devotion and even resources. So, for us, the moment is to come at the moment of primary school, five, four years. Now, we started with five-and-a-half years; we are now starting with three-and-a-half years because of the intuitive nature of touchscreens and so forth allows children of younger ages than the ones in primary school to become involved.

Q: Can you give an example of how it has been implemented on a mass scale?

RA: The first country that took it to heart was Uruguay. At the time the President of Uruguay was Mr. Tabare Vazquez. He's a medical doctor, an oncologist, who even during his entire presidency every Friday in the morning received for free cancer patients in his medical office; even while he was President of Uruguay. This is the kind of human he is.

He understood probably perhaps four words in the dictionary that the rest of mortals don't understand. As a, medical doctor, he understands the word 'urgency'. If medical doctors don't move fast, their patient might die, you know? The second one is as an oncologist he understands the word 'epidemic'. And as a person who has dealt with epidemics, he understands the third word, the desperate need, the agonising need to find the vaccine. And finally, when you discover the vaccine, you vaccinate everybody. You just don't vaccinate one person yes and one person no, thinking that by the law of probability you will probably save the guys who were not vaccinated, because they are surrounded by healthy guys.

Well, Tabare Vazquez came from Davos, from listening to Nicholas, and he told his cabinet, you know, I just discovered the most important vaccine in my life. And everybody knew that he was a medical doctor, so they were eager to see: 'Oh, is it Malaria? Cancer? Tell us, which one is the vaccine that you discovered?' And he said, you know something, I just discovered the vaccine against ignorance and I'm going to vaccinate everybody in my country against ignorance by giving them this thing that I just heard from this guy in Boston by the name of Nicholas Negroponte.

And in 27 months, with their own money, everybody, every child in primary school in Uruguay today has one of our laptops connected to the Internet. It is the most important educational laboratory in the world. Forget about South Korea, forget about Singapore, forget about Taiwan; the country to visit to take a look at what's going on is Uruguay. It is a total transformation of a society. Every child has a computer, even the handicapped children, with autistic children, with Down's Syndrome children, with visually impaired children, even with physically impaired children in wheelchairs, they manage the wheelchairs with the computer.

Q: How would you summarise what OLPC has achieved?

RA: What we have done is really in the words of democratisation, we call it more social equality. This is what five years ago was a privilege; today it is a right. And we have demonstrated that it can happen.

Communications Behaviour

"THE DEMOCRATISER IS THE INTERPRETER FOR THE MASSES – THEY UNVEIL, EDUCATE AND ELUCIDATE WITHIN BRANDED CONTENT AND OWNED CHANNELS.

THEY FOCUS ON THE INFLUENCERS WITHIN THE CATEGORY – AND BRING THEM ON-BOARD AS EXPERTS TO HELP THEM TAKE THE HIGH GROUND IN CONSUMER'S MINDS."

This challenger will seek to create marketing communications that, in the minds of the consumer, 'herald a new era' for this category. That which was hitherto restricted in accessibility is now fully available for all.

The Democratiser will create a sense that this is a new epoch by running a multichannel burst campaign – with the objective to make people believe that 'everyone is being told about this at the same time'.

The messaging will speak at the level of the consumer – so that they can be seen as the interpreter for the 'masses'. Therefore they should take an informal tone. This challenger might also benefit from bringing in celebrities that already have associations that fit with that of a democratiser. They might be used as a spokesperson for the brand – not just within Paid communications but throughout all channels, including PR.

A showcase of consumer reviews or numbers of new customers within the Paid and Owned channels should be used to create the sense that 'things have changed for good'.

The Democratiser should celebrate the people that have switched over – that they have 'seen the light'. This can be achieved through social channels – by retweeting comments – or by putting reviews or even actually customers into the creative that runs within the Paid marketing communications. These individuals can represent the enlightened cognoscenti to the wider audience.

Essentials for the Democratiser:

- Herald a new era with burst campaign that uses broadcast channels

- Speak at the level of the consumer

- Get influencers on-board

- Broadcast your success

- Celebrate those that have switched over

4.
THE IRREVERENT MAVERICK

4. THE IRREVERENT MAVERICK

This challenger narrative is one of provocation, a poke in the ribs, deliberately setting out to create controversy. Irreverent Mavericks are, in effect, counter-culture in a box. There is for most of them no higher purpose or mission than to entertain and engage: they use wit and humour to challenge complacency and the apparent comfort of the middle of the road and political correctness. Their currencies are salience, talkability, the media spotlight. And perhaps an amused gasp of disbelief.

How close to the wind they choose to sail defines whether they genuinely polarise the world, at least at the outset, or whether they appeal to a little of the irreverent in everybody. But they exude the kind of energy and character most of us would like more of: think of the sparkling irreverence of the South African casual dining brand Nando's, for example, or the madcap energy of Scotland's Irn Bru.

Now none of these ten challenger narratives is as shallow as merely a 'positioning': at their most powerful all of them represent, in effect, genuine cultures built around the demands of the narrative they are trying to tell. And the Irreverent Maverick is no different: behaving consistently in this way puts high demands on its own culture – an appetite for the media spotlight, a management acceptance of the downside possibility in taking risk, keeping one's lawyers playing offense not defence, and recruiting for attitude as much as skill base.

There is a temptation to see this kind of attitude as a substitute for product strength – that challengers take the Irreverent Maverick stance because there is no other real difference in product offer between themselves and the competition. But this is too simplistic – very often they have a different kind of product or service proposition wrapped in this irreverent ethos, as the interview with Paddy Power, one of the most entertaining and provocative Irreverent Mavericks today, reveals.

Summary of this Narrative

Core Strategic Thought:
Poke beige in the eye.

What is it challenging?
The complacency and narrowmindedness of the status quo and those who keep to it.

Why does its consumer respond to it? Engagement with its attitude, character and irreverence.

INTERVIEW WITH STEWART KENNY (CO-FOUNDER) AND CHRISTIAN WOOLFENDEN (MARKETING DIRECTOR), PADDY POWER

Paddy Power is an Irish bookmaker founded in the late 1980's. In the 90's it opened its first shops in the UK, and its online business has subsequently been a huge success in Europe. Very few brands have courted controversy as consistently and successfully as Paddy Power – this year, in fact, they created a 'Director of Mischief' as a full time senior position. They pride themselves on treating their customers well, and finding ways to keep the experience entertaining – and the irreverence most visible in their advertising also colours the tone of their product development and customer engagement. A turnover of over 4 billion euros shows the power of their approach.

Interview:

Q: Tell us about how you think of your business.

SK: I think probably the best way of giving it is saying what we did after a year. We just went out openly and said, 'You cannot make money out of gambling. We are not selling that; we are selling an entertainment product'. So we would say on numerous radio programmes …'you can't make money out of gambling. Don't try. This is not what the game's about'. This is about coming into a bookies on a Saturday with £20 in your pocket and having £5 on the horses, £2 on the soccer, £2 on the greyhounds, £2 on Miss World, £2 on who shot JR, £2 on the Simpsons, who shot Mr Burns, and watching all those on television, going home. If you invest £20 in a bookie, the average you get back is somewhere between £17, £17.50. So for £2.50 you are getting your emotional involvement in TV viewing accentuated dramatically, and that is what we were selling; and all we're selling.

Q: Can you give an example about how redefining your business in that way drove your product and service innovation?

SK: We tried to elongate that emotion by saying for soccer matches especially, if you bet on Man United to win 1-0 against, say, Man City, and Man City put a goal in in the first minute your bet goes down. So we would say 'you get your money back if Wayne Rooney scores the last goal of the match'. So you never knew when the last goal of the match was, so it kept your involvement right up until the 90th minute.

Well, once you have that you're in the entertainment business.

Q: How would you describe the Paddy Power brand?

CW: The Paddy Power personality is known as the mischief maker. So it is a brand that is, at its core, very definitely about entertaining people, and doing that in a fun and irreverent way, in a way that friends would do with other friends. So it's the kind of person in the group who's not the joker, but is the one who's got the best banter, and probably takes the piss the most. That's how we think about it.

Q: What started you on your irreverent advertising, and what was your first ad?

SK: Well, they don't come much more politically incorrect than I do. And I've always believed that the vast majority of the population are really politically incorrect, and some of them don't even realise how politically incorrect they are, and really are sick of the thought police telling them what they can think and what they can't. So – remember this was 1990 or 1991 – our first big advertising campaign was [about] the Pope. Outside all the churches, on bus shelters outside churches. Pictures of the Pope with the strap line, 'The Pope to join Glasgow Rangers, 1000-1'.

And there was uproar, absolute uproar. At first I thought 'Oh, I've overstepped the line here', because the telephone buzzed, everything. But we were getting requests for years and years and years afterwards from all over the world, people wanting us to send the ads to them.

Q: How do you know what is and isn't going to strike a chord with your audience?

CW: I think everybody in the business, and it's deep in the culture, has a sense of what it means to make our target consumer laugh, and what it takes to make them gasp in enjoyment: 'I can't believe they've done that'... So it's just having a sense of the people that we're talking to, what resonates for them; I don't know that it's any more complex than that. It's the sort of thing where we sit down and go, 'this is pretty funny, this is something that feels like it's going to cause a little bit of trouble...therefore it's perfect'. There's not masses of testing. There isn't too much internal debate. There's a real kind of sense of, 'Yes, that's a Paddy Power way of doing something'; it's in the DNA, I think.

Q: Do you think you are a polarising brand, or do you think, at some level, Paddy Power's irreverence speaks to a bit of everybody?

CW: I think there'll always be work that goes out that people don't like, because we're always going to talk about things that are… 'taboo' would be the wrong word… but we're going to go after interesting topics – whether it's a referee's decision, or a joke about chavs, there are always going to be a crowd of people who don't like it. But I think for the majority – and we know this from brand tracking work – it resonates, because it's kind of two fingers to authority. Everybody knows that person in their friendship group who is up to mischief and does make people laugh, and always tells the slightly inappropriate jokes. So I think there is something that appeals to everybody. In most cases, when you sit down and kind of discuss the brand, most people start smiling and going, 'Oh, yes, Paddy Power, good on you. You just do the kind of stuff that nobody else would do'.

Q: How do you create an internal culture that genuinely enables, rather than fights this?

SK: We try to get everybody – the lawyers, the security department, the accounts department – to buy into what the culture is. And that culture cannot get interfered with, and the lawyers and the accountants realise it cannot get interfered with. As much as I love lawyers, the lawyers are told 'look, we're going to do this, you just find a way we can do it. If we need to change a few comments in what we're doing, we'll do that'. But if you allow the 'can't because' approach, you get nothing, and it'll take too long. The lawyers are told, 'You've got an hour to tell us how we do this'.

Q: You give them an hour?

SK: Yes, unless we're in a rush! One of the vital things that in my view destroys brands is slow decision making. How can you claim you're an energetic brand if your decision making is slow? It's authenticity. Nobody's going to know that you're slow at decision making, but it's something about the energy that seeps out of an organisation that tells people what it is and what it's not.

Q: How do you think about where and when to take risk?

SK: Financially, we are a conservatively-run company. Legally when it comes to risks in taking bets from certain countries, we're the most conservative of all. But we take risks with our reputation by advertising.

Q: And how do you stay on the right side of that particular risk?

SK: One has to be careful that it is relevant to people's lives and it's relevant to your product. Otherwise they'll think all you're doing is trying to shock. The media won't cover it eventually and people will say it's pathetic. I think that's what happened to Benetton.

Q: How is Paddy Power using the combination of social media and TV now to channel the brand's irreverence and humour?

CW: We are a very conversational brand that people want to engage with, in a high engagement category which is about sport and entertainment. So kicking off the 'We Hear You' campaign, we deliberately made social front and centre, and it was a bit of chicken and egg: we were starting to get people having great conversation on Facebook, and we thought 'That's great, we should do something with that' – and rather than just retweet it or pop it in the blog, we said,' let's really answer it.' So we'll turn an ad around in 48 hours, so that we can do something that is very topical, and therefore, far more impactful than something that had been planned out six months earlier. It makes it pretty stressful, and hard to plan, but it means that everything has a bit more cut through.

Communications Behaviour

"THE IRREVERENT MAVERICK SHOULD PLAN TO BE VERY TACTICAL — BY RESPONDING TO POTENTIAL OPPORTUNITIES. THEREFORE A LARGE PERCENTAGE OF THE MARKETING BUDGET SHOULD BE USED FOR TACTICAL CAMPAIGNS.

THEY SHOULD INVEST IN THE CREATION OF OWNED ASSETS (VIRAL CONTENT PIECES ETC.) IN ORDER TO GENERATE EARNED IMPRESSIONS. CRUCIALLY THEY SHOULD TAKE RISKS. THEREFORE THEY SHOULD BUILD PR AND LEGAL EXPERTISE INTO THE TEAM"

The Irreverent Maverick is an iconoclast. They purposefully do things differently. They are always on the front foot and will often polarise opinion.

Crucially, they take risks. This therefore means they should have senior PR and legal expertise built into the core strategy team in order to ensure that they are ready to deal with the disruption they will cause.

Campaigns should be tactically deployed; therefore a large part of the marketing budget should be set aside for quick-turnaround tactical campaigns.

All creative assets should be housed within Owned channels and they should be easily shareable through social channels to maximise opportunity for distribution.

An Irreverent Maverick might employ the use of humour – this can often be an effective way to shake up a staid category. An example might be approaching comedic talent to help the cause.

And finally, they should keep tabs on how they are doing by monitoring online sentiment towards the brand. If they are polarising opinion, they are fulfilling the role of the Irreverent Maverick.

Essentials for the Irreverent Maverick:

- Crackle with counter-category attitude

- Build tactical activity

- Build PR and legal expertise into your day-to-day team

5. THE ENLIGHTENED ZAGGER

The Enlightened Zagger is deliberately swimming against a prevailing cultural current. They are not simply zagging while the world zigs just for the hell of it; one of the key differences between this and the previous one is the 'truth' that the Enlightened Zagger reveals to us as to why they are taking the stand they are.

Very often this truth is something along the lines of 'the world has gone mad in this particular regard, and I am calling the world out on it'. It is not behaving as a missionary, in the sense that it does not have any sense of higher moral purpose or stature. It is simply saying that 'I know a lot of the world seems to think this is OK, but in reality it's BS, and I am calling it out for what it is.'

We live immersed in a media culture where we are constantly being told how we ought and ought not to live our lives, what we ought to do more of and what we ought to do less of, what is in and what is out. We have television celebrities and lifestyle gurus, the tyrannies of cool on the one hand and productivity on the other, the social imperative of being always this and never that – and an astonishing amount of the world around the Enlightened Zagger seems to fall for it all. But not them.

Unlike the Irreverent Maverick, this stance is not about sticking two fingers up to the establishment, nor trying to move the world on. It is more often in fact about resisting change and defending values now seemingly lost, a deliberate rejection of current trends, behaviours and beliefs. In the interview below, we look at a challenger just starting out on this narrative: Newcastle Brown Ale.

Summary of this Narrative

Core Strategic Thought:
The enlightened brand deliberately swimming against the prevailing cultural or category tide. Often takes low status/ blue collar stance.

What is it challenging? A prevailing and commonly/ unthinkingly accepted aspect of contemporary culture.

Why does its consumer respond to it? Through being provoked and stimulated by the surprising stance the challenger takes.

INTERVIEW WITH CHARLES VAN ES, US BRAND DIRECTOR, NEWCASTLE BROWN ALE

Newcastle Brown Ale was first brewed in the 1920s in the North East of England. A distinctive dark ale, associated strongly with an iconic bottle and label, it was initially a regional beer for local miners. Over time its popularity and distribution grew, and one of its most important export markets is now America. But the US is a very difficult beer market for a challenger to stand out in; as this story starts, Newcastle Brown has only a 0.3% share of what is an admittedly enormous market, yet one which the craft beer revival is only making noisier.

This is a challenger at the beginning of its journey. At the time of the interview Charles van Es, the Brand Director, had only just launched the brand with its new challenger narrative, and was just exploring its potential. But he and his team have dug firmly into the brand's past and authenticity to create a strong and engaging Zagger, calling bullshit on the nonsense they see around them, both in the beer market and beyond – with the intoxicating rallying cry of 'No Bollocks'. Here he talks about the rationale behind the idea, its genesis, and how it is already starting to influence the brand culture.

Interview:

Q: What was the situation you faced?

CVE: One of the first things we did when we started looking at our brand positioning was acknowledging that we basically live in a world of sameness, and sameness comes in different dimensions. Sameness, on the one hand where Budweiser, Coors, the big guys here in the US, their positioning and marketing is very much the same; they bring it in the same way, they say the same things.

At the same time, we are also operating in a very competitive world where there are a lot of craft brands out there – 1,700 craft breweries in the US right now and a lot more coming – and the majority of them make ales like our beer.

So it's very difficult for us to distinguish ourselves. One of the realisations we had is we have to find a voice that allows us to say how we are different from the world around us; I think that was the first piece.

The other piece is that we also learnt from the emergence of craft beer that we cannot just be product-based; we cannot just talk about our beer and how 'our brew is different from other brews' because with 1,700 brews just in the craft space there's a pretty good chance there's something that looks a little bit like us. So we needed a personality, and we started out looking at where we're from and we got to a decent place but then I think we really needed to sharpen it and take it to the next level.

Q: What was the insight that helped you take it up to that next level?

CVE: Together with all the people involved with the brand, agencies, sales and marketing teams, we looked really closely into the history and the roots of the brand and the local culture where we originated from. This beer was originally brewed for hardworking miners and shipbuilders in the Northeast of England. Geordies, the people from Newcastle, are down to earth people, they love a good joke, they don't take themselves too seriously and more importantly they love a good joke.

We want to be that brand that just tells it like it is; to say the things that everybody always wants to say but nobody really does, whatever it is. That all comes together in our belief which is we believe in a world with No Bollocks.

Q: How did you actually arrive at that idea?

CVE: So everybody went out the night before [the brand workshop] to go and find things that we felt were Newcastle-ish moments out there in the world. Gary, in our innovation team, he went out for some reason to a very fancy sports bar – this is New York, there's a fancy version of everything.

He was out in the pub (and in his mind this was just a pub, because he's Scottish), with televisions everywhere, and he went to the bathroom and in the bathroom there's one of these guys that hands out a little towel and puts soap in your hand then gives you a lollipop and then asks for some money. And he was telling the story the next day, and he said 'I was just flabbergasted. What is this? If this would happen in England you'd get beat up. There's a guy handing out towels in the bathroom? That's just bollocks.'

And when he said that we were all sitting in a circle, and there was this realisation, 'That's it – Bollocks. That's the thing we've got to stand up against'. And then pretty quickly we just did a round of 'Everybody tell us a moment that you think is bollocks'. And the moment we knew we were on to something was the moment when we had 25 people there, and everybody had an example. Everybody could point out something in their life where they said 'This is bollocks, and this is why' and for all their own reasons. We immediately had a list of 25 things that people wanted to talk about, and some of it was in their own life and some of it was in the world around them.

That was our 'No Bollocks' moment.

Q: What was one of the first ways you brought it to life?

CVE: Beer advertising goes from dumbed-down stuff to overly pretentious and worthy and that's, for us, an opportunity to call that out and say 'No Bollocks – it's not much more than drinking beer'. So how this came about is I got a call from one of our creatives at the agency on some kind of public holiday saying 'I've got this great idea. I was walking down the street and I saw this ad and we have to do something about this'. It was a Stella ad saying 'It's a chalice not a glass'. That just in itself is so pretentious that we thought why don't we just have some fun with it?

And it was a very simple thing: we just put one of our boards beneath it in line of sight saying 'Who uses the word chalice?' – because no one does. Took a picture and we put it out, we shared it after our distributor conference and within no time, boom, it was out there, it was going around. I got emails from people in Holland saying good luck with the new campaign and we hadn't even sent a press release.

Q: Are you going to stay within the world of beer; is there an opportunity to extend this narrative broader than that?

CVE: I think there's an opportunity for the conversation to become as broad as we choose it to be, however, we choose to start close to home because not a lot of people know our brand, so we need to tell them we have the right to say this.

Q: Has it affected your own behaviour around the brand?

CVE: One of the things that I tried to do is exemplify the belief in the [internal] sales presentation. So this is a sales presentation – people come up in fancy suits and it's all kind of fancy-pantsy stuff and smoke and dry ice and laser shows – and it was a perfect opportunity for us with the brand to say 'that's not us'. I was wearing jeans, sneakers and a T-shirt saying 'Guys, we're going to make this very brief, I've got a couple of things to talk about, we have a new marketing campaign, I hope you like it and goodbye, sell a lot of beer'. And everybody loved it; they were like 'finally, someone is just telling me the truth'.

Q: So this is actually having a cultural influence. There's clearly a distinction here between having a challenger identity like this and a positioning. Can you talk a little about what that difference is for you?

CVE: For me it's all about actually believing in something. A positioning is putting yourself on a map and saying 'This is where I want to be or who I want to be'. What we're doing with this is saying 'This is what we believe in, and if you believe that as well join us, and if you don't, fine – go somewhere else. There are other brands that believe in other things and they're more than happy to take you'. That I think is a big distinction and that helps us.

One of the things we did, as an example, when we enlisted our new agency, Droga5, was that we started out with a manifesto and we just literally wrote down 'Here's the No Bollocks manifesto; this is how we're going to do business. We're just going to tell each other like it is; no bollocks, no saying one thing with another purpose. If you want something let us know. If you agree let us know. If you don't agree also let us know'.

And it's helping us making better work because we can be upfront with each other and if somebody is not upfront we'll call them out in the meeting and say that's bollocks; that's not what we promised to be. Again, we have a long way to go but I think we've really energised ourselves and that's, I think, where you need to start as a team.

"THE ENLIGHTENED
ZAGGER SHOULD CREATE
A DIFFERENTIATED STANCE
BY USING A DIFFERENT
COMMUNICATION TONE
AND CHANNELS TO THAT
OF THEIR COMPETITORS.

THEY SHOULD GO AGAINST THE
GRIP OF THE CATEGORY AND
AMPLIFY THE DIFFERENCE
ACROSS DIFFERENT
CHANNELS."

Unlike the Irreverent Maverick, the Enlightened Zagger bucks a trend. But where the Maverick is iconoclastic with their approach to marketing, the Zagger is iconoclastic with their approach to positioning. The Zagger isn't doing things differently for the sake of moving things on; it is doing things differently for the sake of resisting current trends.

As with any advertiser that serves to radicalise their category, the Enlightened Zagger finds little purpose in imitating their competitors. They should rally against the grip of the category.

Unilever did this with their detergent brand OMO. The whole detergent category talked about whiter-whites – this was the category grip. So OMO launched with their 'Dirt is Good' campaign.

The Zagger should establish the grip of their market and then do the opposite. They should then amplify this across different channels – bringing to life the enlightened view that they have had.

They should Zag across all touchpoints – reimagining the packaging of the product, the store, the people that represent the product, the opening hours etc. They should reimagine everything.

Every touch-point should tell the story that they are different.

Essentials for the Enlightened Zagger:

- Set out your counter-stance with conviction

- Identify the grip of the category

- Amplify your difference across channels

6.
THE REAL AND HUMAN CHALLENGER

6. THE REAL AND HUMAN CHALLENGER

One of the qualities that many challengers share is the ability of the consumer to get a sense of the people behind the brand. They appeal to us at a more personal level than the market leader partly because they are making a human-to-human connection, rather than a brand-to-consumer connection. And the tone of voice they adopt reflects that.

But with this particular challenger narrative the real, human presence of the people behind our challenger is made much more explicit, in its nature and implications; it becomes central, in fact, to what makes the challenger relevant and compelling in this market. As a group of people they are challenging impersonality, challenging the emotional distance a large company keeps between itself and its customers. And by being very explicit about the people behind their brand, about their often deeply emotional relationship with the creation of their product, and their commitment to product and service, this challenger looks to create a much more personal emotional connection. With its greater emphasis on an individual commitment to quality and service, one is given a sense that here is a small and idealistic group of people fighting to bring you something new and good and special, rather than a faceless production factory with a glossy brand front doing what it does to maximise shareholder profits.

As a result these brands become more than just products or services, but compelling characters in our lives. We trust them more, and thus allow them to reach us in ways that we reject from the distant corporate brand.

Historically one saw challengers typically taking this space who were artisanal makers of beer, chocolate ice cream (and the other handcrafted necessities of life). Our interview is with someone whose brand has shown that a challenger can adopt the narrative with an online brand as well, if you are really prepared to overcommit to its implications, and the right culture behind it.

Summary of this Narrative

Core Strategic Thought: A 'real' people brand in a faceless category. Sometimes real people (founders, but not necessarily just founders) visible behind the brand. Often accompanied by the perception of 'small', in stature.

What is it challenging?
The impersonality and facelessness of the market leader or category.

Why does its consumer respond to it? 'At last some real people who understand what I am all about'.

INTERVIEW WITH TONY HSIEH, CEO OF ZAPPOS

Zappos needs little introduction – it has redefined the possibilities of customer service not simply in online retailing, but in any retailing. Tony Hsieh in fact famously describes Zappos as a service company that happens to sell shoes – and builds the culture of the company around a group of individuals encouraged and empowered to deliver 'wow' to their customers. While most companies discourage more than three minutes on the phone to a customer, Zappos celebrates the record for the longest call; with hand-written notes with your shoe order, thoughtful gifts on your birthday, and generous apologies for mistakes, Zappos staff have built a business with a personal connection that grew to a $1.2 billion turnover in ten years.

We went to interview Hsieh in the Zappos offices in Las Vegas, and asked him about how he built such a genuine and human customer experience.

Interview:

Q: How important is hiring the right person, if you are going to deliver an experience like yours?

TH: It's much harder if you are trying to get someone to behave differently from who they intrinsically are. So for us it's really just about hiring people whose personal values match the corporate values, and then every employee is automatically just living the brand, and you don't need to worry about what they're going to do at the bar or what they're going to do on Twitter.

Q: How do you assess whether someone is right for Zappos?

TH: One of our interview questions is actually 'On a scale of one to 10, how weird are you?' If you're a one, you're probably a little bit too straight-laced for us. If you're a 10, you might be a little bit too psychotic for us. But it's not actually what number they give, but more seeing candidates' reaction to it and how they respond to it, because there are some candidates that are trying to figure out, 'okay, what's the right number to say?', as opposed to being honest about it or about what they think.

Our belief is that everyone's a little weird somehow, and it's really more just a fun way of saying that we really recognise and celebrate each person's individuality, and we want their true personalities and creativity to shine in the workplace, and that's whether it's with each other as co-workers or over the phone with customers.

Q: How would I experience this kind of authentic human character in contacting Zappos?

TH: So if you're a customer and you call us, our reps all know the goal is to make the customer happy and develop a personal emotional connection with them. So maybe you call us the first time and you get someone that's really chatty and loves telling jokes and is making you laugh, and that's great. After you get off the phone, you would be wowed, hopefully. Then if you call a second time, maybe you get someone that's not a joke teller, but the person hears, say, your dog barking in the background, and if that person also has a dog, then you can connect on dog-ness or whatever dog owners connect about.

Q: You are famous for the degree of freedom you give Zappos employees to show their human side. Can you give us a sense of how that works?

TH: Employees send flowers for whatever they feel is right. For example, if it's someone's wedding or maybe sometimes we get calls from customers that have to go to a funeral and need shoes for the funeral, they'll send flowers. We had someone who ordered from us, and there was some mix-up in the shipping department, and they were a soldier overseas. I think we accidently shipped them an Xbox or something like that. So they were calling us to figure out how to return it, and the rep decided to just let them keep it, and in fact, went and sent some games, as well, to go along with it just on our own dime.

Q: So how do you ensure people don't go off brand with that kind of freedom?

TH: We don't have scripts in our call centre because we really want people just to be themselves and use their best judgement, and just know that the goal is to develop these connections with customers.

I think a lot of corporations try to come up with rules and policies to prevent certain behaviours, but if you get the right employees, in the first place, and make sure that every employee understands the long-term vision of the company and the brand that we're trying to build, then it's just much easier. Life becomes much simpler, and you don't need all these policies. You don't need to dictate behaviour.

So everyone knows culture is important, and everyone knows customer service is important. The question is, why don't more companies focus on either of those two? And I think it's because they're both longer-term investments. I think the payoff is usually two or three years down the line, and we went through a recession in the last year or two and we, actually, at Zappos, continued to grow year over year, and we're still growing. And people ask us, 'How did you do it through the recession?', and the reason we continued to grow was because of our investments into customer service and culture that we had made two or three years prior to that.

Ultimately, it comes down to financial results, and we've grown from no sales in 1999 to over $1 billion in gross merchandise sales, and we're continuing to grow year over year.

> "THE REAL AND HUMAN CHALLENGER MUST ALLOW THEIR 'MOST IMPORTANT ASSETS' (THEIR PEOPLE) TO COMMUNICATE WITH THEIR CUSTOMERS.
>
> THEY MUST DO IT AUTHENTICALLY.
>
> THEY MUST GIVE A RALLYING CALL TO THEIR EMPLOYEES AND GET THEM EMPOWERED VIA SOCIAL MEDIA TO ENGAGE WITH PEOPLE.
>
> THEY SHOULD SEEK TO SURPRISE AND DELIGHT – AND THEN TELL THE WORLD ABOUT IT."

The Real and Human Challenger should seek to usurp its competitor's crown through a more human dimension to the product or service.

Employees have to be on board. And a social infrastructure has to be in place to support them.

The Real and Human Challenger must give their employees a rallying-call and then get them empowered to engage with people. Social media monitoring becomes essential for them. They should listen to what their customers and prospects say and respond personally and immediately – and then ensure round the clock monitoring and responding.

This challenger should look to take down the boundaries between their people and the consumer – e.g. utilising live events or online tools such as live chat on their website. They should make sure all of their owned channels have the option for dialogue. For example, by building a customer service tab on their Facebook page and responding in an efficient manner to comments on the wall. They should invest in community management and have their first names visible – so that people know that they're conversing with a real person.

Customer service won't always be purely reactive. They should employ a 'proactive' service, such as surprising their customers with reminders, tips or exclusive offers as they seek to surprise and delight. Depending on the category this challenger is in, social media has the power to be a very important communication platform; one that lets their actions do the talking.

From a creative standpoint, they might include testimonials in their ads. If they're especially brave, they might choose to have a near-live twitter feed about their brand on their website or even on digital outdoor. With the infrastructure right, their Twitter feed will be blemish free.

Essentials for the Real and Human Challenger:

- Start from inside your organisation and allow them to represent your brand in social media

- Live and breathe customer service in owned channels as well as social networks

- Provide tools such as 'live chat' and round the clock community management

- Consider customer testimonials in your creative

7.
THE
VISIONARY

7. THE VISIONARY

What is the difference between the visionary and the missionary? The missionary is looking to put a newer, better 'religion' within the category. The visionary, on the other hand, is not setting its sights on tackling something that is wrong within the category – it is actually seeing what the real benefit of its product and service is, far above the functional, and setting a benefit and a future that transcends all the more 'mundane' ways in which the category currently thinks and talks about itself.

So when, for example, the emerging Starbucks in the 90s talked about 'The Third Place' as being that place in your life (between home and work) where you spiritually recharged and reinspired yourself, this was no longer about a mission to put a better cup of coffee on America's table. This was a transcendent vision about the benefits of that experience and what it really represented in people's lives.

More recently Zipcar and Whole Foods would be examples of visionary challengers – Zipcar through its desire to replace car ownership, rather than simply offer a different way of renting them, and Whole Foods through its 'Declaration of Interdependence' – a sense that a retailer (and all of us) needs to have a higher view about the relationship with and between 'Whole Foods, Whole People and Whole Planet'.

The Visionary Challenger below is a new tech company, Lark. Lark is a challenger at the front end of its journey; in the interview the founder talks about how the sense of what the brand stood for evolved from a functional benefit in a piece of technology to something much bigger: the power of sleeping well in all our lives.

Summary of this Narrative

Core Strategic Thought: Sets out higher vision of the brand benefit that transcends category nature.

What is it challenging? The mundanity of the way the category thinks about its (functional) nature and role.

Why does its consumer respond to it? A personal identification with the aspiration set out in the vision.

INTERVIEW WITH JULIA HU – FOUNDER, LARK

L ark started as a device that was a 'better alarm clock' – a vibrating wristband that woke you without waking your partner. But from this product advantage came a much bigger vision: one about not simply improving the quality of how you wake up, but how you sleep – a place to stand with a much, much bigger role to play in its consumers' lives.

At the time of writing Lark was on the brink of gaining distribution in every Apple store, globally.

Interview:

Q: How did the idea for Lark start?

JH: The moment of 'a-ha!' was 5am on a Saturday morning and I had just moved in with my fiancé. We were both workaholics; we were grad students at MIT. He would wake me up every single day at 5am, snooze [through] his alarm clock – you know, beep-beep-beep! And he would do it over and over, and I lost an hour and a half of my sleep every single day, and it was crushing me. And I was already extremely frustrated at myself, at him, and I remember one day, it was Saturday, and 5am the alarm clock goes off and he has to go run, and I was just sitting there like – my life is going to forever be like this.

So I wanted to replace the alarm clock, and I wanted to replace his alarm clock, specifically, not mine; I didn't really care about mine. So that was a moment of truth; how can I re-invent a product that every person uses every day? So I went over to Harvard and there was an amazing woman, Dr. Solet, and she focuses at the Harvard Sleep Medicine Department on sleep and noise. So I started asking her a lot of questions. It's amazing how noise really affects sleep and, especially for women, high-pitched noises affecting our sleep, because we have the baby gene.

Q: Where did the breakthrough come from?

JH: One of the things that we really looked at was: how do you turn the conventional wisdom on its head? How do you wake someone up, maybe, without noise? Is it through smell? Is it through light? Is it through touch? And then we started experimenting and really working on all of these solutions. We had prototypes up the wazoo; a cooling pad, a light bulb, things strapped all over your body, and the needs of the person slowly started to bubble up. We saw that vibration – and specific types of vibration – were very effective. It was a long journey of experiments and we landed on vibration only when we figured out that we could tie it to a phone. So the idea that you could have a secondary object that you're really familiar with power a primary object that no one has seen or heard of or used before is a really powerful enabler. Because we saw that the big trend was from regular home station alarm clocks towards mobile phone alarm clocks. And mobile phone alarm clocks then were a norm for everyday people. So when we found out that we could wirelessly tie a wristband to a norm that was amazing to us. We were creating this when appcessories weren't around, when there were no wireless products that were controlling each other. So it was a really fun challenge and we happened to stumble into being one of the first people who created a bluetooth wireless product that was controlled by an app on your phone.

Q: How did your technical breakthrough become a bigger vision about sleep?

JH: I remember one night, just after we had launched at TechCrunch our idea of a silent alarm clock that woke you up refreshed – and people were loving it, we had a bunch of press, we had a deadline to deliver that product and I remember sitting with my team and saying, 'I think we have something bigger – we're really solving a huge problem'.

One of the top circadian rhythms experts called me up and said, 'Julia, you're doing something that I haven't seen billion-dollar pharmaceutical companies do, which is give one person 30 minutes or one hour more of their most restorative sleep. Drugs can't do that; they can't give you that restorative sleep that's natural to you'. And I remember being so thankful for that glimmer that we were changing the way people slept and that we could, in fact, improve people's quality of life and improve their energy and improve their happiness and improve their relationships with something here, and how do you expand upon that? How do you grow that? How do you grow the message of that?

And so that was the day when I sat down with my team and I said, 'I think we have something so much larger... we have something that can improve what matters to people most in life and that's through sleep; and how do we do that better?'.

I point to that every single time when I talk to my team about our vision. Improve what matters to people most in life, through sleep.

Q: Give us an example of how you bring this vision to life in how you market yourselves

JH: We had been renting some space at the AOL Startex incubator and it was in AOL and Arianna [Huffington] had just become the chief content officer of AOL and was touring the building, and she had just finished a wonderful conversation with all the employees. I just slipped up to her and I said, 'We help people sleep better and it's such an honor to meet you'. And she said, 'Oh, Lark, I've been following you'. And it's great because only she would know who we were because she truly believes in sleeping better for life. So that started a great relationship and a great opportunity to do a collaboration with her. It was all about how do you help little kids sleep better. It wasn't about Lark at all. We created this story about how kids get super powers with sleeping better, and we have some special eyeglasses that help people sleep better. So we gave them magic orange glasses and we worked with eatbigfish on just the touching story that Arianna would share, and she told the story to the little kids with the parents watching. And it was a total blast. Parents would come up to me months later and say, 'Don't know what you did with our kids, but they sleep so much better!'.

It was really the power of story plus science and that's what Lark is really about. It's about combining story and behaviour change with great science. So that was great and then we said, how else can we help AOL? So we did employee Great Wake Up programme, where our sleep experts trained the employees to improve their sleep in a five-week timeframe. It was so exciting to Arianna that she gave us a five-week expose on The Huffington Post at AOL. And the content was so authentic; it was people who had been employees and sleep experts and bloggers talking about their own experiences through the journey. That authenticity was all about sleep, it was never about Lark per se. Certain times it bubbled up about how they used Lark to do this, but it was really about sleep and that consistent voice through the five weeks was really a great time for us to get our name out.

Communications Behaviour

> " THE VISIONARY MUST ESTABLISH AND MAKE MANIFEST THE HIGHER PURPOSE OF THE COMPANY OR BRAND. THEY SHOULD GENERATE A GROUNDSWELL INTERNALLY, ENCOURAGING PEOPLE TO SHAPE THE VISION AND SOCIALISE.
>
> THEY SHOULD ALSO IDENTIFY AN INSPIRATIONAL LEADER OR LEADERSHIP VISION THAT HAS AN EMOTIONAL DIMENSION AND THEN REINFORCE THIS FOR THEM BY COMMUNICATING IT TO THE WORLD."

As the name might indicate, the Visionary comes to power through the creation of something extraordinary. This is not a tale of deposition but one of creation.

The story they should tell through marketing communications must establish and make manifest the higher purpose of the company or brand.

They should start by seeking to generate a groundswell internally. It helps if they have a visionary founder or CEO that galvanises the organisation. If there is no obvious inspirational leader they should establish a powerful leadership vision. This would be a motivating and unifying vision that acts as a point of focus for all within the company. This brand should then encourage people within the organisation to socialise the vision.

For the higher purpose to really motivate, an emotional dimension should be interwoven in to the story – this might take the form of powerful audio visual content pieces about the vision of the company. This theme would run within the marketing communications – so the vision is internally and externally consistent.

By housing the creation of branded-assets within their Owned environments, they should allow their brand zealots to discover it first – so that they propagate out to a wider audience.

Essentials for the Visionary:

- Build a higher purpose

- Start internally – galvanise around a leader or leadership vision

- Build in an emotional dimension

- Invest in Owned channels for zealots – create branded-assets that will be propagated

- Create high impact experiences to dramatise the vision

8. THE NEXT GENERATION

The Next Generation Challenger challenges the appropriateness of the establishment brand for the times we live in today. It challenges the relevance of the past to a new world.

It may be thought that positioning oneself as 'the Next Generation' is simply an executional tactic, not really meriting a place in any kind of overview of challenger strategic narratives at all. But there are specific circumstances which can make this a very strong strategic option for an aspirant challenger.

So we might see challengers looking to use this kind of positioning to profit from, and perhaps accelerate, underlying improvements in its performance as well as shifts in the market context. Eurostar's move to high speed trains allowed it to position itself against the airlines as 'the future of European Travel', through the combination of improved travel times as well as a lower carbon footprint.

Or sometimes the market leader is so popular that one may not be able to challenge it directly head on. Silk Soymilk, for instance, effectively taking on milk itself in the US, faced the problem that this was not a market leader that consumers wanted to see deposed: people love milk (whatever science might say is in it). One can try to reframe and deposition milk in all kinds of ways, but consumers don't want to hear it criticised directly. So adopting this kind of 'next generation' challenger narrative – being 'the new milk' – was a natural one for Silk to adopt at the time.

In the same way in Asia, where status is prized, and very often the Market Leader admired and valued precisely because it is Market Leader, it may be very difficult to take on that Market Leader directly. Far better to implicitly suggest the Establishment Leader is a fine thing – but for the previous generation of needs, or lifestyle, of people; then adopt a 'Next Generation' narrative, and as the challenger, deposition it without overt criticism.

By elegantly positioning the incumbent as perfect for a time gone by, but being clear that time has now gone, the Challenger can position itself as a brand for those wanting to be part of a new generation. That was then, this challenger says, but this is now; new times and a new cohort call for new brands that truly reflect them – and we are one of those.

Summary of this Narrative

Core Strategic Thought: That was then, but this is now. New times call for new brands and services.

What is it challenging?
The relevance of the Market Leader (and perhaps every other existing player in the market) to the modern world, or to the current generation.

Why does its consumer respond to it? 'New times call for new brands, and I as a person am part of the new times'.

INTERVIEW: SCOTT KEOGH, CMO OF AUDI OF AMERICA

Audi of America has been one of the most interesting challengers in the US in recent years. Starting some way back in the US luxury automotive category, a category where social acceptability in brand choice is critical to success, they have capitalised on a flow of strong new products with some of the most eye-catching challenger communications in any category, let alone cars. Their preparedness to take on the larger players, whom they have grouped together as Old Luxury, their recognition that relatively low budgets demand bigger ideas that will create more conversation, their balance between drama and thoughtfulness – all this has led to momentum even in a downturn, and a share of the luxury car market that has doubled, as well as successfully shifting their 'centre of gravity' up towards the more profitable, higher end models such as the A8, A7 and A6. Scott Keogh has been the CMO over that period of growth.

Interview:

Q: What led you to take a 'Next Generation' position against the established luxury brands?

SK: In America, there is BMW, Mercedes Benz, and Lexus, and if you were with them, the world was good. They had high market share, high consideration, high awareness: they were very successful. If you were not them, things were bad.

There had not been a real new luxury brand presented to America in over 20 to 30 years. There've been the same gang of competitors looking at themselves. They were saying the same things; they were targeting the same people; they were bringing basically similar products into the market place, and it was just look at three people staring at each other around a table. And what we really want to do is directly challenge that, and we want to challenge it with our products, with our advertising, with our dealers.

In essence we wanted to tell America there was a day: there was a day for certain brands; there was a day for certain motivations; there was a day for certain buying principles and actions and behaviours... and then of course there's a new day. And I think that's important, because if you're going up against a competitor, or you're going up against a category, if you deliver the same exact messages, and they say they have 200 horsepower and you say 201 horsepower, and they say they have 202 horsepower, you're just going to get a game going on for generations and generations that's going to get you nowhere.

Q: How did you do it?

SK: We positioned an Old World: we positioned a world of darkness; we positioned a world of cobwebs and old rugs and dated furniture and dated ideas; and we opened it up, and we positioned it with light and innovation and technology. And it was a classic 'out with the old, in with the new' strategy. And of course while you had the replacements of grandfather clocks with great LEDs, and you had the replacements of innovative lighting technologies, you also had the replacement of a dated brand of yesterday – Mercedes Benz – by a much more modern, innovative technology of today: the Audi A4.

The car actually was more fuel efficient, and more powerful. It also had LED technology, a host of things that our older competitors just didn't have at the time, and it definitely got the fireworks going.

Q: Did it get the traction you needed as a brand?

SK: Fast forward to today and what happened in the marketplace? Audi now has 60% consideration. We've nearly doubled the amount of people [considering purchasing the brand]. The other thing we've done is we've got the cross-shop. A lot of these competitors' customers, Mercedes Benz and Lexus, and to some extent BMW, did not consider an Audi. And those two things have been rectified. We're getting higher pricing in the marketplace and we are getting a higher consideration. It's exactly what we needed to do.

Q: What's the benefit to a challenger of having a 'Other Surface' to push against?

SK: I think it's extremely important for a challenger brand obviously to have something to push off of, to go up against, because if you don't, you're not a challenger brand. A challenger's always challenging something; whether they're challenging the establishment; they're challenging complacency; they're challenging mediocrity: whatever it might be. And I think for Audi the truth be told, if there's only one thing that we're always challenging and going up against, it's this whole concept of being staid and mediocre. And I think we always modify and tweak that a little bit, but we think in order to set yourself apart it's crucial – whether it's an enemy, if you want to go as far as that, or a whole point of view. Because what that does is it de-positions instantly your competitors, and it puts them into an archaic place, an archaic time. And what it also does is it rallies your organisation around who you are: it gets them motivated, it gets them enthused and gets them excited.

Communications Behaviour

> "DEEP INTEGRATION OF ADVERTISING, SOCIAL AND PR IS ESSENTIAL FOR A NEXT GENERATION BRAND — THE MARKETING MUST APPEAR TO BE MORE THAN JUST ADVERTISING — IT MUST FEEL CULTURALLY RELEVANT. THEY SHOULD SEEK TO CREATE A SENSE THAT THIS IS A NEW EPOCH. THEY SHOULD SEEK TO INVOKE THE HERD MENTALITY IN ORDER TO MAKE PEOPLE BELIEVE THAT 'EVERYONE IS MOVING ON'.

The war waged by the Next Generation is an intellectual one. It seeks to state that if you haven't moved over to us yet, then you have misunderstood something important, or more specifically, you haven't understood how things have moved on.

This is a case of new versus old, so the marketing communications must reflect this. The Next Generation challenger should take a fresher and more modern approach to their competitors. But perhaps more importantly, they should make sure they integrate the disciplines of advertising, social and PR so that the marketing feels as if it is more than just advertising – it should be a news story.

The brand should build on this by leveraging the behavioural economic principle of social proof – where people are attracted to this brand because everyone else is. By seeking to invoke the herd mentality they will make people believe that 'everyone is moving on'.

In order to achieve this they should use media that feels like it is being seen by everyone – even if it isn't. For example, large billboards or online homepage takeovers could be used to create the perception that this message is being seen by all and that 'everyone will know about this'.

Owned and Earned environments can play a key role in activating the herd mentality – encouraging people to engage and then broadcasting the amount of engagements achieved across the Paid, Owned and Earned channels.

Essentials for the Next Generation:

- Signify a moment in time that marks out the new epoch

- Integrate the disciplines of advertising, social and PR – creating news stories

- Select media channels that help people think your ads are seen by everyone

- Broadcast how many people are engaging with your brand across Paid, Owned and Earned channels

9.
THE
GAME
CHANGER

9. THE GAME CHANGER

When a Challenger Brand sets out to be a Game Changer it isn't simply setting out to challenge category convention (like its Irreverent Maverick or Next Generation siblings) but to go further. Their explicit ambition is to change the way we think about and experience their category, through our relationship with their product and service.

The brands that have this capability– often rooted in experiential, functional technology Challengers– typically present us with products and services that not only change the way we think about a particular category, but go as far as to change the way we live our lives altogether, in big or in small ways.

Becoming a Game Changer is not something you can simply intend to do or something you must convincingly announce. It is something you have to do. This stance, perhaps more than some of the others, is not about taking a point of finding a new way to communicate your story or your ambition. It is less about identity and engagement and more about dramatising the experience. It is an entirely new product, service or experience, wrapped in an entirely new category narrative.

And once you start changing the category, you need to keep changing it – or someone else will change it again for you. The only way to stay ahead is to think like the hungry Challenger you once were. Ask Wii.

Summary of this Narrative

Core Strategic Thought: A brand and product with an entirely new perspective on the possibilities of a category, which invites the consumer to participate in the category in a whole new way.

What is it challenging?
The fundamental drivers and codes of the category to date. Not the beliefs or values – more the dimensions of the consumer experience it has played up and played down.

Why does its consumer respond to it? They are engaged by fresh perspective on a familiar market: 'Wow, I'd never thought of this experience like that before'.

INTERVIEW WITH CHRISTOPHER LUKEZIC, DIRECTOR OF MARKETING AND COMMUNICATIONS EMEA, AIRBNB

Airbnb is changing the hospitality business. At one level it is a practical alternative to hotels – instead of booking a hotel room Airbnb allows you to book accommodation in an apartment belonging to someone who lives in the city you want to visit: good quality accommodation without having to pay hotel prices for hotel services you don't need. At another level, though, it is fundamentally reinventing the experience of travelling, building around the concepts of community and trust, as Christopher Lukezic shares in the interview below.

Q: How would you describe Airbnb?

CL: Airbnb is a global marketplace for unique accomodation. It allows anyone who has extra space that they're looking to rent out to travellers to do so. At the same time we've made it simple and easy for travellers looking for unique accommodation and experiences to be able to book anything at any price point anywhere on the globe. We have a presence in 19,000 cities and 192 countries around the world and currently offer over 150,000 properties.

Q: And how did the company start?

CL: Airbnb was founded in 2008 in a San Francisco apartment in the SOMA neighborhood of San Francisco by two former RISD graduates – Joe Gebbia and Brian Chesky – who were both looking to launch their own startup. With a pending rent increase threatening their potential eviction, they decided on a whim to monetize the extra space in their apartment by renting three air mattresses to goers to the IDSA Industrial Design Conference, which was happening in San Francisco that year. The experience of hosting strangers from around the world was transformative and the idea stuck because the people who they ended up hosting weren't the typical people who you would expect to be hosting under such circumstance. They ended up being mostly middle-aged design professionals from all over the world, some had families with kids, and all were very successful people. What they realised was that the social interaction they had during that time had a profound impact that lead to the realisation that accommodation could be more than a commodity, but could actually be a part of the travel and the social experience of being in a new city and I think that stuck. So what's evolved from three air mattresses on the floor of an apartment has now expanded to 150,000 properties, from private apartments to private islands anywhere you could imagine going in the world.

Q: What do you think your main challenge is? What's your ambition?

CL: Our primary marketing focus is on building a community not a brand. The entire company is focused on this mission, so we've eroded the definition of 'marketing" within our organisation. I think we are redefining what a community means to a brand, what it means to a company, and our customers. And, for us, it's around this idea that our business is rooted in trust. It's rooted in bringing people together around the globe, and that goes beyond marketing a product. Our focus and mission has to reach beyond our website and beyond our product in order to touch something fundamental and emotional in our customers lives.

Q: Obviously, your main competition is hotels or the hotel industry in general. Do you have a point of view about those as your competition? Or do you tend to not talk about them at all?

CL: Often times the easy comparison is to compare us to hotels, but I think that isn't how we view our business. What we're doing is bringing a different viewpoint, a different design ethos and experience to travel. As a company, we direct our focus back onto our users and solving problems for them because, ultimately, we're a service more than we're a product. There's this shift – partially caused by the economy and partially generationally – that has people seeking value and experience, something that we're able to offer. People are getting excited about the new possibilities afforded them through travel and they are sharing their passion with those around them; it's happening very naturally and organically. Most of the time we're not actually responsible for those unique experiences; the host on the other end, who's offering the accommodation and providing the hospitality to the traveller, is often times the force behind that, which then goes on to have a profound impact when people from different cultures are meeting and directly exchanging.

It's no longer a corporation making this possible; it's another person, whether they're in Paris or India or in the US. Airbnb is simply the catalyst to make these connections possible. The social impact of this is quite powerful.

Q: Do you see yourselves as creating a very new kind of experience?

CL: There's a great anecdote that our CEO has used a number of times that best illustrates this. Brian, when he told his mother about this business model, she said, 'there's no way I'll ever do this.' And his grandfather said, 'of course, that's the way I used to travel.' Only in the post WWII industrial boom do you see hotels really emerge as the primary accommodation option. In that era we started to see a homogenisation of products and services, which included hotel rooms; and I think that's what people wanted at the time. Over time, I think that's shifted. The internet is connecting people and cultures.

For instance, people going to Paris no longer want to stay in a generic space – they want to actually experience Paris the way that it was built, and part of that experience is staying inside an apartment in Paris, away from the tourist attractions. I think that's something that we're offering and making possible for millions of people, but it's certainly something that's been offered for ages, before hotels.

Q: Do you see anything in particular with Airbnb that made it unique, that really created the breakthrough?

CL: Yes. We emerged first and set the stage for what has happened with social travel and the emergence of the sharing economy in general. The main reason for our success is that we've taken a very long-term vision and a very long-term approach to building a brand, building a company and community. If building a brand takes a few years; building a community takes decades. Early on we knew that the ultimate success of our business would come from building a community, not merely a brand. That required us to use a decade-long approach to building the business, without being distracted by short-term gains. This approach allowed us the chance to make sure we were doing the things, day in and day out, that would better the lives of our users.

A few years ago people thought that this business model was crazy. No one would have thought this was possible, but we've proved that it was, and that people really wanted this. We think differently, as most leaders of successful businesses do, but we also act differently and we structured the mission of the business to always put our users front and first, often times doing things that don't scale and don't have immediate measurable returns. It wasn't about putting up billboards and running advertising campaigns to get lots of users very quickly, because we had to take a long-term and slow approach. We have had to build trust with our members one-by-one, often times by meeting them in person.

At one point no one thought anyone in the world would go and stay with someone in their home – that was such a scary idea for many! However, by starting slow and learning from our customers along the way we've proven that this is something that people want to be doing and it's something that is not only offering them economic value but also an incredible social and experiential value that for many has fundamentally changed their outlook on the world.

'THE GAME CHANGER SHOULD
BUILD COMMUNICATION WITH
OPINION FORMERS TO ALLOW
FOR THE OPTIMAL FLOW OF
INFORMATION. THEY SHOULD
CELEBRATE THE PRODUCT
OR SERVICE WITH HIGH
PRODUCTION VALUE CREATIVE
WORK. THEY SHOULD POSITION
THE PRODUCT/SERVICE AS A
MAJOR EVENT. THEY SHOULD
ALSO CONSIDER CELEBRATING
THE DESIGNERS/INVENTORS
BEHIND THE PRODUCT/SERVICE
– AND THE BACKSTORY."

Of all the challenger models, the Game Changer is the one most focused on product. The product does all the talking. The product is the story. The governing principle for Game Changers in communications behaviour is to be unashamedly proud of their product – as opposed to the Irreverent Maverick who is unashamedly proud of their marketing.

The Game Changer will want to open up and romance the product design or story to the world. This might involve eulogising about the origin of the idea and the journey from conception to realisation. It may also point towards explanations as to why and how the experience is better. Every touchpoint should offer the potential consumer an idea or story that gives a fresh perspective on the category.

The Game Changer will be highly selective about the environment in which their products are seen. They should create contexts that signify change and help propagate the idea of marking out new space for the consumer.

A technique of the Game Changer should be to celebrate the new products/services that they launch as major marketing events, building up to the launch as if it is a significant moment in the calendar and annual calendar and in national life. Activities that suggest to people, who experience the game changing product, that life as they know it might never be the same again.

Because of the importance of building drama around the product, the owned environment will be crucial. Paid channels, if deemed necessary, will guide people towards these environments as part of a wide-scale design to open up the story. Earned communications will concentrate on high impact publicity. Social media presence will build in keeping with consumer interaction and understanding; the Game Changer should assure that the product alone can alter consumer expectations of the entire category.

Essentials for the Game Changer:

- Put the product at the centre of everything you do

- Carefully select your media environments, always opt for dramatically different context

- Don't feel you have to go out of your way to engage consumers, let the product shine

- Behave with the restless passion of a brand that is constantly improving

10. THE FEISTY UNDERDOG

The Feisty Underdog is what many regard (misleadingly, as we saw at the beginning of the book) as the classic challenger stance, in part because Avis and The Pepsi Challenge, those two iconic challengers, both fit so famously this 'David vs. Goliath' model. It is a perfectly valid narrative – we just need to remember it is only one of a number of challenger narratives at our strategic disposal.

The challenger that does adopt this narrative, though, aims to reduce the world to a binary choice – creating the emotional illusion that there are just two brands for the consumer in a category to choose between. It offers at least an emotional reason to support the underdog (they root for the combination of our inferior stature on the one hand and our chutzpah on the other), and perhaps a rational product or service one as well.

In doing so, in comparing itself explicitly to one other larger player, it attempts to radically simplify consumer decision-making in the category. Challengers don't succeed by increasing choice in a category, they succeed by reducing it – reducing choice (implicitly or explicitly) to a decision for the consumer between the old or the new, the quiet or the loud, the sensible or the exciting. And in the case of the Feisty Underdog, the bias is for explicit comparison, certainly inside the company and usually outside as well, and a comparison can help highlight their own virtues. And the strategy can obviously extend to drawing the Market Leader – and the Market Leader's communication budget – into that public conversation as well, and using the bigger player's media dollars to give salience to the challenger's own ambitions, and the conversation they want the category to have.

Many Challenger Brands start out as the Feisty Underdog – firstly, because it is a position in which they genuinely find themselves and, secondly, because playing up to it seems like a dynamic way to accelerate salience and conversation around its offer, and get some of the available audience on its side. For obvious reasons it is not a narrative for the faint-hearted, and while with time and success we see many challengers subsequently migrating to another narrative, there are few narratives that energise the internal organisation as powerfully for an ambitious challenger as this has the ability to do.

Summary of this Challenger Narrative

Core Strategic Thought: Stick it to Goliath.

What is it challenging? The dominance of (and unthinking consumer preference for) the market leader.

Why does its consumer respond to it? Everyone loves an underdog – Oh, and given the choice between those two options, that does look like one to try...

INTERVIEW WITH TIM WRIGHT, COMMERCIAL DIRECTOR, KING OF SHAVES

King of Shaves is a male grooming brand, rooted in shaving products, that is an energetic and vocal challenger to the gigantic Market Leader that is Gillette, and the passive Number Two of Schick/ Wilkinson Sword. Twenty years into their challenge, King of Shaves still very deliberately adopts the narrative of the 'Feisty Underdog', explicitly calling out the Market Leader, and drawing attention by contrast to King of Shaves' own, fiercely competitive value proposition: always looking to offer '50% more'.

Here their Commercial Director, Tim Wright, talks about why he believes this challenger narrative is such an important part of their armoury, and how to keep the consumer and the retailer on your side while you are using it.

Interview:

Q: Tell us a little about King of Shaves

TW: We're the number three shaving brand in the UK and in North America. We are in both parts of the shaving business, what we call software and hardware. We started in the UK 20 years ago, and over the years we've grown and grown into a business which has become recognised, I think, as the challenger brand in the personal care market. There are not actually that many challenger brands in the whole of the personal care and health and beauty category. There are a lot in women's beauty, like Benefit and those types of make up brands, but in the men's market, there are very few. I think that's traditionally been because men buy toiletries in a very rational way and so, consequently, the emotional approach has been, I think, under-utilised – with the exception, of course, of the market leader in fragrances, Unilever's Axe, and more recently Old Spice.

Q: What is your value proposition relative to Gillette?

TW: We have always believed that it's not just about the headline price of the pack, it's about the individual price of the shave. We've always had a policy of offering 50% more. So while the standard pack for Gillette is a four-pack; we always offer a six-pack. When Gillette sells its razor handles it supplies them with one blade, whereas typically we supply ours with three. So we're offering better value

Q: Why do you explicitly compare yourselves to Gillette as part of your challenger strategy?

TW: The reason we have always believed that we can be what you would call a Feisty Underdog is because we've had such a beast to go after [in Gillette]. In the US they still have nearly 85% market share of razor blades, which is phenomenal, and probably is the last remaining consumer package goods monopoly that's out there.

I've always believed that if you want to be black, it's really important that the brand you're going after is white, because the contrast between the two is exaggerated, and can be exaggerated. Certainly when we originally looked at 'how do we take on Gillette', the thing that we always believed was missing from everything that was part of the brand was humour. There was no humour, there was just seriousness around Gillette that had supported their 'snap-on tools' approach to shaving, which was purely functional, driven by car ad-type shots of 'This is really tough, you're a tough guy, we're a tough brand'. Then the whole metrosexual thing came along and people said, actually, you don't necessarily have to be so tough.

At that point we believed that if we were to be successful we needed to do two things. One, we needed to go in the completely opposite direction – be funny, be irreverent, be contrasting ourselves to that. And two, we needed to acknowledge they existed. These guys are so big – it's just such a massive monopoly that they have.

Q: Give us some examples of the kinds of things you have done as a feisty underdog to the 'beast' you call Gillette.

TW: We did our 'Shaving Bonds', where we asked the consumers to fund our advertising campaign so we could beat Gillette, and that ranged from investing in our business so we could fund our advertising, right through to [our event at] Speaker's Corner. We did a big campaign at Speaker's Corner where we did speeches about how brands were terrible in operating the monopolies and they were ripping you off.

We did [a website called] The Best Your Dad Can Get.com, and that was about Gillette, and then we decided that we wanted to go one step forward, so we actually registered another domain which is The Best Your Granddad Can Get and that's Wilkinson Sword.

As you know, we spend a lot of time on Twitter – Will King, our founder, spends a lot of time on Twitter too, and the feedback from people is that they really do feel as though we're the consumer on their behalf standing up to this bully, and a huge proportion, an overwhelming majority of them want us to succeed against them. Probably they see the way we do it, they enjoy the humourous way we're trying to do it, rather than just frankly saying, 'they're expensive and we're cheap'. Because clearly when you're looking to shave your face, you're still requiring a lot of trust to put a piece of razor-sharp metal against your face.

Remington is our partner in the US and traditionally has been up against some fairly substantial brands like Philips in its core business, and they've got something over there called the Remington Value Model, which really is about pitching products at the right price, particularly as their major retail partner is Wal-Mart. One thing which we and Remington were encouraged to do by some of the key retailers in the US was to point out the comparison between the price points of 'Seriously?' and 'Honestly!' – 'Seriously?' being $22.99 for Gillette ProGlide Power and 'Honestly!' being $11.99 [for our razor]. That campaign was run on TV and radio over there, and that's been really well received. The laws in the US, as you know, are completely different in terms of comparative advertising.

Q: How has the economic situation been affecting this kind of comparative strategy for you?

TW: This period of austerity for us, it's not been a head wind. It's been a wind that's really blown well behind us, that has given us the opportunity to say, well, 'you do need to re-evaluate every single purchase and that includes razor blades'. So we've been lucky, I think, in some ways that that's taken place.

Q: Have the retailers always responded positively to the way you present yourself alongside Gillette?

TW: One of the big issues that you do face [if you take on a market leader like this] is that no retailer on this planet wants to see the cash margins they enjoy from Gillette going south: they're a substantial part of any global retailer's non-food business, probably the largest part of any supplier in their non-food business, whether that's in Europe, US, Asia. The percentage margin is weak, but the cash margin is very strong; these products have got a very high price point.

So what you're looking for is market growth, and we've always been able to argue that we've been able to bring people into a higher priced item from a lower priced item, typically because we have a disposable razor category which sits below where we operate, and we have been fairly successful in dragging people out of that, effectively trading them up in the static, old-fashioned, trade-up model into the higher price point, but in doing that delivering much stronger gross margins to the retailers.

We've always been very careful that, whilst being the feisty underdog, we have to have, effectively, a two-pronged message strategy – one B2C and one B2B. The one that's B2B has to be very careful to say 'We're not here to disrupt your pricing model in terms of the value that you manage to extract from Gillette as a supplier – they're too important. What we are here to do is enhance that.'

Also, it's always been said to me, outside of a formal meeting with a retailer: 'We need feisty underdogs to keep such strong establishment brands in check'. If not, they start dictating terms to the retailer which become completely one-sided and the traditional healthy balance which exists between a strong supplier and a strong retailer starts to get really uneven because of the monopoly existing. Obviously a lot of retailers are also completely paranoid that they may become complicit with the monopoly. Particularly with European anti-competitive laws now, they need to be very careful and they almost need to be able to demonstrate that they've gone far beyond just bringing other suppliers and looking at other opportunities, and show that they're willing to bring in competition and healthy competitors where that's appropriate.

Certainly we play to that too by saying to the retailers, we're offering you something you can't get from Gillette in terms of the brand and the proposition and the unique design of the product.

Q: So how does this affect the way you think about media?

TW: Certainly we play to that too by saying to the retailers, we're offering you something you can't get from Gillette in terms of the brand and the proposition and the unique design of the product.

Inevitably mass media is very challenging for challenger brands because when you've got a big spender, a monster spender, as we've got [with Gillette], then I think [as a challenger] you're literally spending nothing. You're better to spend nothing than you are to spend ten, £15 million because when they're spending 500 you're wasting your time. You really are wasting your time. You're in the valley of doom.

Q: What results are you seeing now, 20 years on?

TW: Well, in the UK we've leapfrogged Nivea and L'Oréal, so we are the number three overall men's grooming brand behind Gillette and Lynx, so we have a strong share in the UK. We haven't been in the US for so long, but we're in all major retailers. We have obviously partnered with Remington. Our market share in the US is still only 3% market share, but, as I said before, it's a pretty monster market and we're up against the guy that's got 85 to 90%.

So there's still a lifetime of work to do. I'd describe it as a lifetime of work to do.

Communications Behaviour

> "THE FEISTY UNDERDOG
> SHOULD COMPARE AND
> CHALLENGE THROUGH
> BROADCAST AND EXPERIENTIAL
> CHANNELS – ALLOWING FOR
> THE AUDIENCE TO BE
> A 'JURY'. THEY SHOULD KEEP
> A TACTICAL BUDGET FOR QUICK
> TURNAROUND 'EXPOSING' OF
> OTHERS SHORT-COMINGS.
> THEY MUST BE RELENTLESS
> WITH NEW MESSAGES AROUND
> TACTICAL OPPORTUNITIES."

The Feisty Underdog should seek to compare and challenge through broadcast and experiential channels – allowing for the audience to be a 'jury'. Making direct comparisons with the competitors in the category will allow the Feisty Underdog to elevate its importance quickly.

Any comparison made between their brand and the category leader is healthy debate, so they must not be afraid to take them on, even if opinion is divided. Ultimately it will be this debate that provides a distribution channel to reach a wider audience – through the creation of Earned content.

This should be further fuelled through a significant investment in proactive community management – everything should be engaged with and retweeted.

The Feisty Underdog should also encourage people to comment or vote on what they think – and then consider showcasing this within their marketing communications. This could take the form of a voting mechanic within an Outdoor campaign or carrying out bespoke research about how people are feeling about the other companies in the market and turning this into a PR story – which they could use to reference within a tactical campaign.

Budget permitting, the Feisty Underdog should seek to engage their competitor wherever they land. They must call them out on their dated practices with their own marketing communications. They should really try to get under their feet, and chip away at them. They can afford to be very opinionated and disruptive; they play the role of the much younger sibling with the arrogance of youth but with a fresh perspective to boot.

Essentials for the Feisty Underdog:

- Pick on the category leader and single-mindedly focus on their shortcomings
- Compare and challenge them
- Seek people's opinions and broadcast them to all
- Constantly look out for tactical opportunities

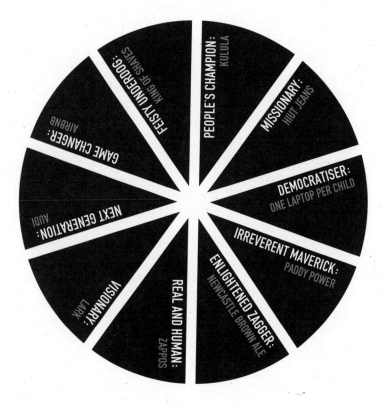

PEOPLE'S CHAMPION:
KULULA

MISSIONARY:
HIUT JEANS

DEMOCRATISER:
ONE LAPTOP PER CHILD

IRREVERENT MAVERICK:
PADDY POWER

ENLIGHTENED ZAGGER:
NEWCASTLE BROWN ALE

REAL AND HUMAN:
ZAPPOS

VISIONARY:
LARK

NEXT GENERATION:
AUDI

GAME CHANGER:
AIRBNB

FEISTY UNDERDOG:
KING OF SHAVES

SUMMARY: THE TEN STANCES

11.
USING THE MODEL

11. USING THE MODEL

This is a piece of work designed to go beyond theoretical typologies, and offer instead a practical strategic framework for those for those who want or need to challenge something about their category to succeed. Our desire is to help challenger leaders, teams and brands structure their strategic and communications approaches in a way that genuinely drives breakthrough – as well, perhaps, as stimulating critical questions about the different kinds of internal challenger culture and leadership that will be required to sustainably live in each of these narratives during the time it will take to make it a success.

So this chapter will explore three different ways in which the model can be powerfully used. They are clearly only three from a much broader range, but are different enough and common enough to offer marketers and business partners some insight into where the model's value for them might lie.

The three we will touch on here are:

i. Launching into an emerging category

ii. Relaunching in a crowded category, that already includes other aspirant challengers

iii. Maintaining one's momentum as a challenger

i. Launching into an emerging category

We've all been in this situation – we see a growing category, perhaps 2-5 years old, a bunch of brands piling in, and we want to challenge for a piece of it, too; a big piece. Where do we start?

The first step is to understand the dominant category narrative. By and large, a fast-growing category adopts the narrative of the challenger that started it – so energy drinks are invariably Irreverent Mavericks, because Red Bull is an Irreverent Maverick, and every other entrant subsequently took this narrative up as well. In smoothies, every brand is real and human, because the defining smoothie brands in the key markets adopted this position so successfully in building their consumer base that every subsequent entrant – and most of the own label players – simply did their best to pile in behind them. And the consequence being, of course, that if one really wants to be a challenger in this already bustling market, the last narrative you now want to take up at this point is the one that the leader and those fast followers are using.

So what this model offers us, in effect, is a way to fast track an exploration of nine different challenger narratives to explore instead, and use some of these other narrative types to stimulate some initial possible routes to explore.

Perhaps we could start by asking ourselves.

- What are the four narratives here that seem most intuitively powerful for us within this emerging category, given the nature of the category on the one hand, and our own product and cultural strengths on the other?

- What would it mean for us to challenge the category in the way that each of those narratives demands?

- What if one of the classic brand examples of each of these narratives were to launch into this category: how would they approach it? How would they aim to drive awareness, conversation, trial and share?

- What kind of communications behaviour would be most important to them? What behaviours would convey the narrative with appropriate intent and urgency? What environments or context can narrow the gap between the story and consumer experience? What communications strategy would they pursue that overthrows the current journey?

If we really lean into the implications of these four questions, one or two of those first four narratives we initially focused on will probably fall away — they won't appear to be as relevant to this category, or support what makes our product experience potentially different, or may even be too culturally difficult for us to authentically sustain.

But what potential lies in the remaining two or three? And what would it mean for us to really lean into adopting each of those challenger narratives and make it succeed?

As a brand? As a culture? As a leader of that culture?

ii. Relaunching in a crowded category, that already includes other aspirant challengers

If the category is of any size, and with more than three players, the chances are today that there will already be another brand in there styling itself as a challenger. This doesn't mean we can't challenge the market, simply that we will have to do it in a very different way, using a very different kind of narrative.

Now the narratives challengers take are of course not always quite as clean as the above descriptions suggest – we have pushed them apart here to make the differences more apparent. In the real world, one will often see a challenger leading with one narrative, but introducing a healthy splash of another – a desire to be the People's Champion, for instance, flavoured with the attitude of an Irreverent Maverick.

Nevertheless, we are going to map what those competitive narratives are on the model on page 81 and explore which of those narratives is already taken within the category at the moment.

We then have two options. The first is to pursue an approach like the one in the section above, playing out four potentially interesting challenger narratives, and seeing which one bears the most promising fruit.

The second is to really question which of those stances we mapped out is genuinely taken. We might want to regard each narrative 'slice' in the image as a scale, with 0 in the middle and 10 on the outside of the circle. Many of the players in our category adopting one of these will be half-hearted; their culture won't allow them to embrace the full opportunities of that narrative, their product or service experience may not live up to the story they would like to tell, their business partners are not fully on board – there are any number of reasons why they might be engaging with it at a fraction of the intensity they could do; clearly wanting to take up a stance of that kind, but executing it at a 3 or a 4 on our crude scale.

But challengers are all about execution, intensity and theatre, and one of the opportunities we need to consider in a crowded category is a narrative where we can live at 9 or 10. What would it mean, then, to not just adopt that challenger narrative, but to offer a much more intense and vividly expressed version of that challenger narrative than anyone else in the category? Would that allow us to genuinely own it in a way that the pretender can't? What could we do in terms of the product or service experience, for instance, to take the interest the competitor has generated in that approach and turn it into an on-ramp for our own potential growth?

iii. How a challenger maintains its momentum

Each of the stances above represents a different kind of challenger story to tell. Within each of them the brand and the people behind that brand are in effect telling us why they started, and what they are trying to do. We come to know what they are struggling against, and who their enemy is. In some we even get a sense not simply of their beliefs, but of their hopes and their fears – for themselves, for their category, for the world at some level, and for us. The anthropologist Bob Deutsch commented that people often thought that Bill Clinton's success with the electorate, in spite of the various scandals that attended his presidency, persisted because people just liked him; Deutsch's observation was that this was not actually the case – that the reason his success persisted was not because they liked him, but because people felt he liked them. The same is true with many of our challengers: we feel at some level they like us. We are not just target markets and demographics and share objectives – they share their stories with us, and invite us to participate with them in realising them.

So why do challengers move between these stances? What is the benefit? In part it is about refreshing the way one presents oneself to the consumer – stopping yourself becoming just another part of the brand landscape once the consumer has become familiar with you. Staying stimulating, interesting.

In part it is about discovering new and fresh sources of challenge and conflict from which to renew your own story, and create fresh sources of 'Grip' on the imagination of the consumer. One might argue that there may also be a more significant kind of evolution here – one might suggest that some of these stances represent 'higher order' positions, offering deeper kinds of emotional relationship and identification, that challengers naturally evolve up to.

So we have seen Southwest moving from being, in effect, a 'real and human' airline to talking about 'Giving America the freedom to fly' – evolving its narrative to that of a Democratiser: opening up to Americans of all income groups the ability to use air travel. Staying within the airline business, Virgin Atlantic moved from an Irreverent Maverick phase at launch (capitalising on the existing Virgin image) to evolve in effect to a People's Champion narrative. It is still irreverent, of course, but it has looked to take more of a 'high ground' narrative.

Underpinning all of these is the recognition that a challenger needs to keep moving to stay the same: what made it fresh and engaging is not what keeps it fresh and engaging. As it succeeds in achieving one goal, or overcoming (really or apparently) one struggle, it evolves its narrative, and public ambition, and moves onto the next.

Which in turn helps with the other key requirement for a challenger, both in terms of internal culture and external relationships, namely to be never seen to win.

Being a challenger is, after all, about a state of mind, not a state of market.

A state of mind committed to perpetually overthrowing the order of the category in an unreasonably short space of time, for a maximum return on energy and investment.

POSTSCRIPT

If you want or need to explore the thinking and tools around these Ten Challenger Narratives further, you can do it in two ways. If you'd like to know more about the research behind it, you can see videos of the interviews at www.eatbigfish.com. If you'd like to look at the strategic possibilities with eatbigfish, please email adam@eatbigfish.com.

If you would like to explore further the communications behaviours your company or brand should be considering, please get in touch with us at PHD Worldwide. You can do this by either visiting us at www.phdww.com or emailing us canwehelp@phdww.com.

With Thanks To:

Rodrigo Arboleda

Heidi Brauer

David Hieatt

Tony Hsieh

Julia Hu

Stewart Kenny

Scott Keogh

Christopher Lukezic

Charles van Es

Christian Woolfenden

Tim Wright

Helen Redstone

Emma Wood